Guide for the Journey Home

A P'taah Transmission

DEDICATION

This little book is dedicated to all who are sharing this wondrous adventure called Human Life Now. We hope you find it useful in your journey Home.

CONTENTS

ACKNOWLEDGMENTS

Thanks to Jennifer Luckman Carter and
her creative editorial team who made
this book possible.

1 GUIDE FOR THE JOURNEY HOME

As you go about your daily life, you employ the skills you have acquired since childhood to make life work for you, to survive and hopefully be successful in your endeavors.

For most of you this can be more or less of a struggle. Often, just when you think you are winning and the pieces of your life are working, it seems that the universe pulls the rug out from under you and you are once more left floundering.

The truth is that everything is always changing. No matter what, you will always have challenges to meet and what seem to be negative situations to resolve. There will be times when you have to deal with grief and loneliness. There may be times when you feel like an utter failure, when you wonder if life is really worth living.

Our desire for you is that you learn to dance on the moving rug called Life—not only to dance, but to dance with consummate skill, elegance, passion and grace. Our desire for you is that you become more and more of who you truly are, that you stop struggling and fill your life with joy and laughter and play.

What keeps this from being a reality is simply your beliefs—who you believe you are and what you believe about yourself in your world. The first step in changing your reality is to change your beliefs, to come into the absolute knowing that you are the one who creates that reality. It is you who has that power. No one else has power over you except for the power you give them. You create your reality absolutely. Your exterior life is whatever you perceive it to be.

Until you understand that you create it all, you cannot change it. You are a victim of your own beliefs. When you see this, you know that if you do not like what you have created thus far, you may change it. When you see this, you begin to comprehend the awesome power that you are. The more you begin to consciously create, the more powerful you become.

This requires that you become more focused and pay more attention to what you may have previously dismissed as "coincidence" or "accident" or what you call "good luck" or "bad luck."

There are no such things. Nothing is random. Everything is creation and co-creation. Everything in the multiverses is a Thought in the Mind of Creation. Everything is spun out in an incomprehensible web of connectedness from this Unified Field of Consciousness through infinite dimensions of time and space.

As human beings you create yourselves in your multitudinous lifetimes as threads or bodies of energy and consciousness existing in the Unified Field of Consciousness spun out from the greater part of you. These clumps of energy are what you might call soul energy. We call it the light beingness of you. If you had eyes to see, you might call them "angels!"

This soul energy that you are sends out in a most joyous and creative way many, many of these threads of consciousness to experience human existence. And all of these lifetimes are occurring at the same time.

So although you, of course, experience everything in a time-line, what you call past or future lifetimes are, in fact, occurring Now. They are created in and from the Unified Field of Consciousness outside the space/time continuum in the same way everything you perceive in your world is created. Everything in your physical reality is created from the Unified Field, all of it connected, all of it a magnificent explosion of consciousness.

Everything in your world, every atom and molecule, whether you perceive it has life or not, is a body of aware-ized consciousness. It may not be a consciousness that you recognize, but it certainly has its own awareness. Everything you perceive in physicality exists first and simultaneously in the Unified Field before it can be manifested into physical existence.

Because everything in existence is connected, everything impacts everything else. Your thoughts and emotions are energy and consciousness that impact and change everything they touch.

Thoughts do not live in your head. They are like radio waves that are broadcast into the universe. You can direct your thoughts, wrapped in emotion, to anywhere in the seen and unseen realities. They are not constrained by time or space.

In this fashion you can see that nothing is separate from you. If you want to experience connectedness to your soul, to your loved one who has died, or to a tree, even to a place, of course you may. Be still. Breathe. Be the thought and be the love and just listen.

When you understand the connectedness and the impact you have upon your world, the power that you are, then comes the responsibility of that knowledge. Knowing that your thoughts and feelings may either enhance or pollute, you are then required to take responsibility, to pay attention.

As we have stated, everything in physical existence first and simultaneously exists as a body of energy. Your consciousness affects matter. All change and transformation is effected first in the non-physical. So your non-physical thoughts first impact the energetic body of physical matter and the change is then manifested into the physical.

As you go about your day-to-day life, everything in your environment is affected by what you believe and how it feels. When you are happy and energized and lavishing loving care and attention with thanks and gratitude on everything around you, something extraordinary occurs. Even that which you call inanimate objects respond. If you had ears to hear, you would sense a kind of hum. It is a song that sings of the pleasure in joining with such a beautiful resonance of Beingness. It is not about *doing* anything really; it is about *being* the thanks, the gratitude and love. Our desire for you is that you may do everything in your life in that state of being.

So we are giving you perhaps a wider perspective on who you really are, your universe, and how you create reality, even when you do not consciously do so. As your awareness expands and your knowledge and understanding of the power of you grows, so does your ability to create what you desire in your life.

It is a game, you know. This life was not designed to be a punishment. It was designed to be a most outrageously creative game, without limits, for you to express your immortal, divine sparkle in physicality.

2 ALL IS ONE

Each of you reading these words has a passionate yearning deep within the breast of you to come Home. Each of you fervently desires to become whole, to live your life in peace and harmony. You desire to find fulfillment and contentment and to truly know more about love.

But you have forgotten who you are. You have forgotten your power. You have forgotten that you are truly Gods and Goddesses come forth from the Unified Field to play in this realm called Earth. To be outrageously creative in the day-to-day manifestation of these, your human lifetimes. To nurture your planet and everything upon and within Her.

You have forgotten that you are beloved and that love is the truth of you, that you are supported in every moment by the Universe, if only you could allow it. And you have forgotten that Love, this truth that you are, is just another name for Goddess/God, All-That-Is.

You are lost in separation and isolation having forgotten that you choose to come, lifetime after lifetime, simply for the adventure and emotional experience of it all.

The ultimate truth of you, the most expanded description of you, is that no matter what the situation or how you feel, you are in every moment a Perfect and Eternal Expression of the All-That-Is.

No matter how alone or how divided you feel from other people, from Goddess/God, from the universe that surrounds you, you are not separate. Everything that exists in the multiverses exists as a manifestation of the All-That-Is.

The life force of existence is that spark of Divine Creation, without which there is no-thing. It is this spark that unites existence in the seen and unseen realities. As we have said, even the things in your physical universe that you regard as lifeless have a molecular structure imbued with this aware-ized consciousness.

You exist here in a physical embodiment which allows you to physically experience your physical world. Much of the time you feel that your existence stops at the outer limits of your physical body, which can reinforce the feeling of separation. However, the more expanded view of you shows that you exist as a vibrational frequency, a body of energy or consciousness, which wraps around and binds with your physicality, allowing you to be the human person you are.

Your body is a miracle indeed. Every atom and molecule, every cell, every organ, has its own consciousness linked to every other portion of your body. Every cell and every organ also is connected to every like cell or organ in existence. Your body, in a way, is part of the Earth herself. It resonates to all things of the Earth. When you die, your consciousness moves on and your body returns to the Goddess Earth to which it is intrinsically bound. At a physical level you are connected to every other physical manifestation.

The non-physical reality is where the greater part of you resides. The consciousness of you is the eternal part of you. It is that portion of you linked to your greater Self or soul energy. It is your direct link to the Unified Field of Consciousness or the Void of Creation from whence comes every possibility and probability of manifestation in the multiverses. It is the "soup" of creation, the place, if you like, where all knowledge exists.

Even your physical body exists mainly in the non-physical. The knowledge and memory of your DNA, your molecular and cellular memory, is stored in the Unified Field. There is nothing in your physical reality that does not originate in the Unified Field.

So what links everything in the physical and non-physical realities is this spark of Divinity. As you expand in awareness and use your astounding powers of focus and attention, you will more and more find yourselves able to consciously connect with both the seen and unseen realities. The desire to connect and the acknowledgement of connectedness will transform your world. The more you use this ability, the more it is.

As you connect, you have more awareness of the validity and rightness of every living thing, animal, vegetable and mineral, and in fact as much of the universe as you can perceive. So you grow in compassion, in gratitude, and in awe and wonderment of this astounding oneness.

You indeed are awesome jewels of creation and everything wondrous that you behold in your natural world is there, in a way, as a reflection to you of your own unique beauty and wondrousness.

Our desire for you is that you will more and more come to feel the connectedness and oneness of all creation so that you may live in more joy and spontaneity.

3 THE LIE

For generation after generation you have believed The Lie. The Lie tells you that you are unworthy and guilty creatures, filled with sin. It says that there is a God who will judge and punish you and that if you do not do this or that, you are unworthy of God's—or anybody else's—love and unworthy of any of the wondrousness you might imagine for yourselves.

The Lie includes the idea that to be worthy you must live life adhering to certain practices, rites or rituals according to the society in which you live. And you are given some picture of the "finished, perfect, ideal person" you could become, if only you could get it right.

Well, the truth is you are already perfect and you will never be "finished" because you are perfection unfolding unto infinity. How is it that you, who are a Thought in the Mind of Creation, a Perfect and Eternal Expression of Source, could possibly be unworthy?

This Lie which has been planted in the collective consciousness has been, and still is, a most powerful tool of manipulation and control.

Fortunately you as an individual are more powerful than the collective consciousness. The fact that you are all connected means that as you grow into a more expanded conscious awareness, you assist the expansion of all of your species. The Lie then becomes powerless.

Each of you is an awesomely powerful spiritual being, creating and co-creating your day-to-day existence. No situation or experience has any significance apart from that which you give it. However, as you begin to live in freedom and joy learning the truth of who you really are, then you negate The Lie and show by your example the greater possibilities.

One of the most insidious results of The Lie is that you grow from early childhood with the belief of your own unworthiness and this belief creates a separation within the self. You grow up trying to hide those things that you judge about yourselves. You cannot love who you are and until you can, you are doomed to a life unfulfilled.

In this time when there is an explosion of information, there is much given forth as "truth." In fact it is really more of the same old Lie. Even much of the so-called new spiritual teaching is locked in this box of how you "should be" in order to step into your own knowing.

Enlightenment itself is held up as a prize you may win if you follow this or that practice, this or that discipline. It is therefore necessary for you to learn discernment so that you are not caught up in the fear of getting it wrong or missing the boat. We tell you that Enlightenment is simply the natural result of loving who you are as an Extension of the Mind of Source. This is Truth.

You are, no matter how it seems or what the situation is, a Perfect and Eternal Expression of Source. You already exist as an enlightened spiritual being. It is called the soul essence of you. You are here in this reality because you chose it at soul level simply for the emotional experience.

You are existing simultaneously in multitudinous human lifetimes and they are all occurring in the eternal Now. You also are experiencing lifetimes beyond this planet and beyond this plane of existence. In a way it is a game of wondrous creativity, however it is one you have forgotten how to play.

This being so, if anything is stated indicating that you are less than a Perfect, Eternal Expression of Source, then this is not your highest truth.

If anybody states that you must or should do it this way or that way or you will not be worthy or that you will not become enlightened, you may know that this is not your highest truth.

If anything is fear-based, it is not your highest truth.

Refute The Lie! You are worthy of all wondrousness simply because you exist.

You know, it is time that you also started to really trust your feelings in these matters. When you are contemplating new material or listening to somebody else's ideas, you may apply the same criteria, but also pay attention to your feelings about the material. The deepest part of you knows rightness. It feels comfortable. If you are feeling uncomfortable ask yourself, "Is there any fear attached to this?".

4 CREATING YOUR REALITY

This is Truth—you create your own reality absolutely and in every way.

Most of the time you have no idea that you are actively creating your day-to-day reality or how you are doing it. In the same way that all of creation is linked, so too is every part of your life a co-creation in the most amazing and complex way.

At soul level you choose to incarnate into a human life form. At this level you choose your family and your genetic heritage. Very often you choose a grouping with whom you are interacting in many other lifetimes and time frames, choosing different roles in most incarnations.

You choose your time and place of birth, your gender, your race, your nationality, your socioeconomic situation and the broad spectrum game plan of your life. This game plan is loosely the matrix or structure within which you will make your life choices day by day.

Within the matrix, you choose probable realities. It may be that you set up a probable reality that one or both parents die when you are still very young or perhaps they may divorce.

It may be that you birth yourself with a passion for music or painting or mathematics. It is interesting to note that where there is this talent or passion, it may manifest in many lifetimes to a greater or lesser degree. Also that groups of entities sharing the same interests may come together just for the fun of sharing the interest or passion. In this way you may recall a situation something like, "Oh so-and-so loves to play violin and his great uncle was a noted violinist."

We have heard many of you ask, "If it is true that we create our own reality, why would any of us choose to be born into a family where we are abused or where we would starve to death or be born into a time and place of war?"

It may seem to you very callous if we say, "Simply for the experience of it," however, contemplate this. You are truly eternal creatures. You incarnate into the human experience hundreds and hundreds of times, not because it is a punishment. You choose it because it is the most wonderful, astounding, vibrantly intense, emotional experience.

Each lifetime simply is like an in-breath and an out-breath to the eternal soul. And at soul level you desire to create every possible experience and emotion.

Now, having set up the game plan, you are ready to be born. From the moment of your physical birth, you begin to garner the human experiences which teach you, in a way, who you think you are.

These early experiences set up a belief structure. And the emotional responses to these beliefs, coupled with your interactions with your family and their own beliefs, are the framework within which you create your day-to-day life. By the time you are around six years of age, those beliefs and the emotional response to them are more or less cast in stone until such time as you choose consciously to change them.

Many of your beliefs are held within the collective consciousness as "truth" or "immutable fact," and most of you are not even aware that you hold them or even that they are not necessarily true.

So these beliefs are the cornerstones of your co-created reality. However, as many of you have found, thought patterns by themselves do not necessarily create or change your reality. As we have said very often, if you could create change simply by thought alone, your world would be a very different place.

So what is the power that creates your reality? E-motion, energy in motion, which is the reason you keep incarnating.

It behooves you to really understand that the Universe supports you 100% of the time. It supports you without judgment. It allows you to create whatever and however you may.

This being the case, we suggest you quickly learn how you may consciously create your life so that you may create more peace, harmony, love and joy. And create it not only in your own life, but because you are all connected, in the entire world.

To become more consciously creative is not really so difficult. You are required to:

- Pay attention to your thoughts and reactions. Where either may be negative, you need to deal with the fear underlying those thoughts.

- Pay attention to what you believe about yourself in and about any situation and change those beliefs that no longer serve you.

- Learn how to be what you desire for yourself. We shall give more detail about these a little later.

Love and fear are at the opposite ends of the emotional spectrum. Much of your life you spend in neutral. You go about your day-to-days not paying too much attention to your thoughts or feelings. Much of the time you are focused on your past or future rather than paying attention to Now.

Your emotions are the power and the driving force of your creative life. The more intense the emotion, the greater the creative drive. The most powerful emotions are love and fear. Now we have said that the Universe supports you 100%, without judgment, so if the underlying emotion driving your choices and decisions is fear, then the Universe will support that.

If your underlying belief is that you are unworthy of love, that belief creates the fear that you will not find love. The Universe will support that emotion and belief and will assist you to create the people and situations in your life that reflect your fear and belief.

Many of you are afraid of what supposedly hidden fears and beliefs you might have that could influence your life in a negative fashion. However, we say to you that nothing is really hidden. Your life shows you exactly what you believe about yourself and your world and how that feels. If you are unhappy with some areas of your life, ask yourself, "What do I believe about myself in this situation?" Now reflect upon the parts of your life that bring you joy and ask the same question.

Pay attention! There is no such thing as "accident" or "coincidence." Everything you experience is a co-creation.

When you understand that each one of you is a sovereign, powerful being co-creating your individual life and that you are totally connected one to another, then much of the blame and recrimination will fade from your life.

Conversely, many of you shoulder blame and feel guilt about situations without acknowledging another person's sovereign participation in the co-creation.

Where there is a situation, perhaps a car accident resulting in injury or even death, the outcome may emotionally affect many people—the families, the friends, the people who may have witnessed the accident, the doctors or nurses who perhaps attended the people who were in the car. In this case you can see that it is a co-creation which may have far-reaching effects, far beyond the people initially involved in the "accident."

Whatever you create, whether you judge it to be positive or negative, is a gift for you. There is some wisdom to be garnered, something more for you to know about yourself or your world.

Sometimes you may find a situation grievous or horrific. It is for you to know that there is a pearl there for you, an opportunity for expansion. Perhaps an opportunity to reach out to someone and, in so doing, discover a gem you did not know existed.

So indeed, it is a wonderful game you all play. Our desire for you is that you learn to play it with consummate skill and have loads of fun as you do so.

Pay attention to the results of your conscious creations. Give yourselves a pat on the back and say "thank you" to your Goddess/God Self and to the Universe for the privilege of being here in this, your miraculous world.

5 THE NOW

If the seat of your power is your emotions, the place of that power is in the present or Now moment. Your past is gone; your future will be created from the choices of this moment.

We cannot emphasize this enough. The more you learn to pay attention and focus on what is occurring in your mind, in your body, to your reactions and feelings, to what is occurring outside of your self, the more you will find yourself in the flow of your life rather than struggling against it.

It is in the Now that you catch an old belief, one that perhaps you didn't even know you held. Perhaps this belief no longer serves you but it holds you imprisoned in an old negative pattern. When you recognize the belief, if you could stop for one moment and tell yourself, "No, that is no longer my truth because I know thus and thus." If you then replaced that belief with a more expanded truth, you would find after doing this a few times, the computer of your mind replaces the old with the new.

The Now is your place of transformation. You know, when you laugh, truly laugh from your belly, you are totally in the present. No past, no future. When you find yourself in laughter, joy, passion or fascination, you go with the flow of it. In that immersing of oneself in the Now of the fascination, you create a space or channel through which information or knowing can flow.

Where do you think "original thought" originates? When you are in the joy of Now there is no negative judgment, at least not at that moment. You often castigate yourselves for enjoyment after the event!

Choices and decisions made from this Now space carry the same resonance. So it is that then your life is lived mainly in peace, joy and harmony.

However when a situation provokes a reaction of fear—anger, aggression, resentment, jealousy, etc.—the opposite occurs. Instead of flowing with the feeling, everything in the belly tightens and you hold on to that energy. Eventually, those stored feelings create illness and disease and a blight on life itself, throwing you off your center point of balance and harmony.

If you were to deal with all of the fear-based stuff as soon as it occurs, in the Now of it, you would very quickly come back to your center point. You are then ready to make your next choice or decision from that place instead of from the resonance of fear.

When you look at it logically, you can see how important it is to pay attention Now. Your body speaks to you all of the time. It tells you what it needs in the way of nourishment, rest, exercise, etc. You miss the signals if you are not aware. You miss moments of joy and reflections of beauty if you are not in the Now. You miss opportunities to give and receive love and play and camaraderie, to give nurturing and compassion and even simply time.

In the Now you catch yourself in negative judgments about other people. Understand that there is nothing outside of yourself but an opportunity to know more about you. A negative judgment about someone else is based on a negative thought or fear you have about or for yourself.

All of this is moving you toward knowing more about who you are and dealing with the limiting beliefs and fear which keep you from loving who you are, keep you from the life you desire and the life you deserve.

6 FEAR

The polarities of energy—Love and Fear. We will speak of this, as we have spoken of it for many years, because it is a cornerstone of life on this plane of reality. It is what governs a large percentage of your day-to-day reality, your choices and decisions. It is what keeps you stuck.

When you birth yourself into this reality, you come forth initially remembering who you really are. You remember that Home is the Unified Field of Consciousness where all is one and love is the only reality.

For a time after birth the consciousness is not very focused in the third dimensional plane of reality. It feels very restricted and unable to communicate in the tiny physical body it finds itself within. Very soon, however, the focus becomes anchored in the physical and in the timeline you have chosen, and the memory of "elsewhere" begins to fade.

In spite of being loved, usually, the baby-you finds that with the inability to communicate, your needs are not necessarily met when required. It feels that love is being withheld and that baby-you feels powerless to change things. Before very long the infant, then the small child, learns modalities of behavior to earn love or to get what it wants. You learn that if the child, the little-you, behaves as you feel, you are not acceptable, not loved and not worthy of love unless your behavior is "appropriate."

You are also taught that the world is a dangerous and perhaps scary place. By the time you have reached the age of six years, you have been given negative reinforcement around 60,000 times.

You also come to believe that love equals pain. Where someone you love punishes you or leaves you or dies, a part of you feels you have died of the pain of it.

On top of this there are the belief structures of the collective consciousness, much of it fear-based, and the belief structure of the familial unit. Much of the belief structure of the familial unit is not necessarily recognized as such. Sometimes it is simply "the way we have always done things." Sometimes it is superstition or religious beliefs or rituals. These are the things that help to shape your life. If these beliefs are fear-based or ideas that reinforce the belief that you, or humankind in general, is unworthy, then this becomes part of the matrix from which you create your reality.

By the time you are about six years of age, the beliefs you have about who you are and who you are in your world have become fixed. You grow up physically and mentally, but within there is still the child, the baby one, who believes, "I am not worthy" or "I am not enough."

And this little one mostly controls your life! By this we mean that every time you make a choice or decision in your life that is fear-based, it is that little boy or girl in control, not the rational free adult.

In saying this, we hasten to add that not all fear is negative. In certain situations, of course, fear and the compulsion to respond to it may well save your life. However, to have one's life ruled by fear is to be in prison. It means that you can never reach your full potential or allow yourself to be who you truly are.

That little person who lives within you is the judge and the controller. She/he loves you absolutely and will do anything to keep you safe. In a way every time you push down the fear, you are denying and abandoning that portion of you hidden away since childhood.

When you are joyous, you flow with the feeling. When a situation provokes fear you try to control it. You hide it or hide from it. You sweep it under the carpet and hope nobody else knows about it. It is not safe to be vulnerable. You cannot afford to reveal who you think you are because others will judge you and find you unlovable or worse, you cannot show your heart else someone might put a knife in it.

So you may say that the little person inside each of you is named Fear. It is not evil or terrifying. It is not your enemy. It is that portion of you who has forgotten the truth, has forgotten who you really are.

Our desire for you is that you will learn to transform the fear into love, to become all that you can be.

7 TRANSFORMATION

Basically all of your fears stem from the belief that you are unworthy. However for you to be able to more easily identify your fears in order to transform them, we have broken them into four categories, the Four Basic Fears:

1. I am unworthy (not enough)

2. I am powerless (to change anything)

3. Love equals pain

4. My world is not a safe place

It is only you who has the power of transformation. You create your own reality absolutely. If you do not like what you are creating, you have the power to change it.

The first step in transformation is to take responsibility for your own creations. For as long as you see yourself as a victim, you are powerless to change anything. You are not a victim and no matter what the horror story, you are at some level a co-creator in the event.

Remember the importance of the Now. It is your power place, the place of transformation. The past has gone. You only have Now to choose how you will be, who you will be, and that choice will create your tomorrows.

You can only transform fear whilst you are feeling it in the Now moment, otherwise it is just an intellectual exercise. As we have already discussed, if you could change everything by simply thinking about it, your world and you would be very different indeed.

The feeling, the e-motion, is the power that creates your reality. The transformation of fear to love can only occur while you are feeling that emotion. Emotion itself is simply energy. It is you who labels it or creates it as "good stuff" or "bad stuff." So in essence what you are doing is changing the frequency or vibration of the energy by your intent. This is how powerful you are.

The only way you can transform the frequency is by embracing it. You have tried to suppress it, to get rid of it, and it doesn't work. You have tried to ignore it and pretend that it isn't there. It doesn't work. You can only acknowledge, accept and embrace the feeling in the Now moment to transform it. Remember, what you invalidate, you empower!

So here are the Four Keys to transform those fears into love:

1. Take responsibility—acknowledge and accept that this is your fear

2. In the Now

3. Whilst you are feeling it

4. By the total embracing of it

Of course, it's a little difficult to embrace the fear when you have spent your entire life running away from it. However it is truly not too difficult.

First simply stop. If you are amongst others, take yourself off to the bathroom or wherever you can be alone—just for a few moments. This is not some lengthy, agonizing, roll-on-the-floor situation. It is a simple exercise of the heart.

So, stop. Then consciously breathe—deep, comfortable, even breaths. You know, everything in your physical world is really a metaphor for the greater reality. In your world breath is life. In the greater reality life is the Source. When you stop and breathe with intent, you will immediately connect to your Source-self, your Greater-self. And as you breathe, you will feel your self begin to feel balanced and centered.

Then imagine your baby self, aged perhaps four years, perhaps a little older. However you see yourself is appropriate. There is the little one standing in front of you, lonely, terrified and heart-broken.

What is your reaction? In your mind, you reach out and take this little you to your breast. This little one has struggled all the days of your life to protect you and make sure that you survive, this little you whose name is Fear.

But what have you done with fear, always? You have hidden it away, denied it and swept it under the carpet

So perhaps you would say to the baby you as you hold her/him close, "Thank you for loving me and looking after me. I'm so sorry that I abandoned you all of those years ago, but I did not know any other way to be. Now I do know, and I will never again abandon or deny you. We are together forever, you and I, and together we are Home. Thank you. I love you."

And you will hold the little one and breathe, saying your "Thank you, I love you" and just be. Nothing to do. Just be.

As you do so, the Goddess/God light of you swirls that energy of fear into the light of Itself and the fear is now transmuted to love.

And lastly are the Four Steps of Transformation or the Baby Me tool:

1. Stop and breathe

2. Imagine the little Baby You

3. Hold this little one to your breast

4. Say "Thank you. I love you!"

Sometimes we hear you say, "Oh, that is just your imagination!" However, we would impress upon you the understanding that the imagination is truly a most wondrous tool of the soul. If you can imagine something, then it exists—not necessarily in your third dimensional reality, but nevertheless it does exist.

You can use your imagination to create a space within whereby you may accomplish many things of great benefit, as well as the transformation of fear. We will speak more of this later.

8 JUDGMENT

The ultimate transformation occurs when you can wholeheartedly love who you are in the heartfelt recognition that you are a Thought in the Mind of Creation, a reflection of the All-That-Is, perfect and eternal. What keeps you locked in your box are the negative judgments you have about yourself. As we have said many times before, no God could or would judge you as harshly as you judge yourselves.

We hear your internal dialogue. We hear how you judge those things about yourselves that you think no one else knows. We hate to remind you, my beloved ones, nothing is hidden! We know how you have been invalidated in your life and how that has set up a program within you of guilt and negative self-judgment. We hear how you are not clever enough, beautiful enough, successful enough, young enough, rich enough, etc., etc.

You can see that all of this is about lack, and lack promotes fear—the fear that you are not enough. Much of the time it is just too painful to look at the things you think you are not. It is much easier to project the judgment (fear) onto people and things outside you.

So next time you find yourself in a negative judgment of someone, just pause and ask yourself, "What am I afraid of?" Because we promise you that there is a little something inside to look at, some little issue that requires your attention.

Do not confuse negative judgment with discernment.

Negative judgment makes something wrong. Discernment says, "I honor your right to be as you please, but this is not my choice."

Also, we would say, it is appropriate for you to defend the weak and those unable to look after themselves. It is for you to follow your heart in all things.

We remind you that there is no judgment from on high. The Universe supports you and whatever you sow, so shall ye reap. You do not need a God to judge and punish you. You will do that very nicely yourself!

The more you identify those fears and beliefs that you keep locked in your little box and that keep you from contentment and joy, the more compassionate you will become. Strangely enough, every person you meet has exactly the same fears as you. Every person has that heartbroken little one tucked away inside. Some of you are just more adept at hiding it.

So when you witness appalling behavior and man's inhumanity to man, indeed decry the behavior and the inhumanity, but take a moment to think about what created it.

Love is the truth of you. Everything else is an expression of the fear of lack, including your judgment.

9 ABUNDANCE

The Unified Field of Consciousness, of which you are an expression, is a place of infinite possibility and limitless creativity. It is a Field which knows no lack.

Love is the ultimate abundance and fear the ultimate lack. You, as human, are created from the abundance of the Unified Field. You come forth as creatures of astounding creativity and power, capable of creating more love, joy, happiness, laughter, and contentment than you can at present imagine. All of this is called abundance. You are the abundance. It is your truth.

Abundance is not something you go out and get. It is who you are, or who you are not. If it is who you are not, then you need to look at the beliefs and feelings that keep you separate from your own greater truth.

Apart from identifying those limiting beliefs, it behooves you to pay attention to how often each day you reinforce the perceived lack in your life. Also look at how often the idea of lack limits your life. How often may you have said, "I would love to do this and that, but I cannot because I do not have the money." The moment you have said it, it is your truth and the Universe will support that.

A more unlimited way would be to focus on what you want to do and to know that you, the powerful creative being that you are, have the power to create what you want. Much of the time you do not even have to know how you will do it, only that you will.

The Universe supports what you focus upon, where you put your attention. The more you focus on "have not" the more you are being the resonance of lack and that is exactly what the Universe will support. You will create more and more situations to show you who you think you are.

We have said that it is all about being the abundance. So how can you be that resonance which is abundance? Again, pay attention! Look about you. Do you see each day the abundance of nature? The abundance of beauty? Are you basking in an abundance of good food, a comfortable bed, warm clothes when needed? Do you have people to love, friends and companions who care about you? Do you hear wonderful music, the song of birds and the warmth of the sun on your face?

All of this is abundance indeed. Now, when you give thanks for the abundance, really feeling the thanks and gratitude, your heart expands and fills with joy. You are in the vibrational frequency of abundance. You are being the abundance.

This frequency aligns with the Unified Field of Consciousness which supports you absolutely and so you co-create more of what aligns with that frequency—more abundance.

Let us look at the idea-construct you term "money." Many may say that money is not "spiritual." In fact many of you have such issues around the idea of money and spirituality that you do not, where possible, even use the word "money." You use the word "abundance" as if "money" is a dirty word. And then you wonder why you have no money!

We would say there is nothing that is not spiritual. Money is a wonderful quantifier in terms of abundance because it is immediately identifiable. Either you have it or you do not.

If you are one of the multitudes who bemoan the fact that there is not enough money, look at the negative beliefs you may have around money. Many of those beliefs relate to things you may have heard as a child.

- Money is the root of all evil.
- There is never enough money.
- You have to work very hard for your money.
- Money is never there when you need it.
- Money doesn't grow on trees.
- Rich people are bad people.
- The rich get richer and the poor get poorer.
- Our family has always been bad with money.
- Good (or spiritual) people shouldn't (be seen to) be interested in money.
- I am not clever enough to have money.
- I am not worthy.

So, any or all of those beliefs will certainly bar the flow of money to you. Take note of how many times in a day you re-affirm your ideas of lack.

Also, you think of money as something separate from you. But what is it really? Money is an idea-construct. It is a symbol of energy. Much of the time you hardly ever handle physical money any more. It is simply numbers on a computer screen.

So really money is energy. What are you? Energy. Energy is energy. So what keeps you separate from the energy called money are your beliefs and the feeling that those beliefs engender. It is only you that keeps you separate.

Once you have identified those beliefs that keep you in lack, then it is to pay attention to those thoughts that are produced by the beliefs when they pop into your mind. Old habits in thinking patterns need to be changed. So when a thought comes up, "It is always such a struggle to pay my bills," stop!

Remind yourself, "That is no longer my truth. I live in an infinitely abundant universe and money flows to me without struggle."

When you receive money, any money, whether it is your pay packet or a penny you have picked up from the floor, say to yourself, "Money always flows to me. Thank you, thank you, thank you." This is such a good game!

Remind yourself that money is energy which must flow. You are energy that must also flow, creatively and positively. The energy of money and the energy of you may merge together to create wonderful things. Imagine that you really bank at the Universal Bank of Infinite Abundance.

Another important component of abundance is that of gratitude and thanks. You may say that gratitude and thanks are likened unto a conduit to your own soul energy and thusly to the Unified Field. It is like a connecting rod. You are opening to flow.

If you begin each day with thanks and gratitude, in a way you set the vibrational frequency of the intention for the day. In opening your heart with thanks, you open your heart to receive more of the frequency of the abundance of all wondrousness.

We have a little Thank You song that you may use each day, or make up one for yourself.

Thank you for the love that I AM.
Thank you for the love in my life and
Thank you for the love that surrounds me.
Thank You.
Thank you for the miracle of life that I AM.
Thank you for the miracle of life I see reflected all about me.
Thank you for the gift of life.
Thank you for this perfect body, my health, my well being.
Thank you.

Thank you for the abundance that I AM and
Thank you for the abundance I see reflected all about me.
Thank you for the riches and the richness of my life and
Thank you for the river of money that flows to me
and through me.
Thank you.
Thank you for the beauty and harmony.
Thank you for the peace and tranquility.
Thank you for the wonderment.
Thank you for the Joy.
Thank you for the passion and curiosity and fascination and
Thank you for the privilege of serving and
sharing the gift that I AM!
Thank You! Thank You! Thank You!

We promise you that if you were to sing this song each day, with your heart, your life will change. It is very good to sing this (make up your own tune) whilst you bathe your body in the warmth and deliciousness of running water. The crystalline structure of the water is like a magnifier. However, you may simply say the words any where and any when, as long as your heart is involved. This is being the abundance.

People have asked, "Who are we saying thank you to?" You are saying thank you to the greater beingness of you, to the Universe, to Goddess/God and to everything that exists, for being part of your wondrous creation called Life.

10 RELATIONSHIPS

What a wonderful game this is. What a wonderful reflection it is to you about who you think you are.

You may say that your relationships start with the relationship you have with you. Relationships really mean all of your dealings with other people, not only those with whom you are intimately acquainted.

Of course it is also necessary to look at the idea of "intimacy" too, because too often in a marriage or partnership or even friendship, it simply does not exist.

Many of you have created wonderful relationships and you have worked out what works for you. Where you come into a relationship from a place of wholeness and sovereignty, you will create a different relationship than one based on the fear of lack.

If you are ruled by the idea that you are not worthy of love, honor, and respect, then you will create a relationship that reflects that truth. If you believe that any marriage or partnership is doomed to failure, then you cannot expect otherwise.

Some of you create self-perpetuating stories of betrayal or violence. In other words, what you may have experienced perhaps in childhood becomes the "truth" of relationships for you.

For some what you seek is someone to provide you with what you feel you lack. That may be money, social position, someone to look after you, someone to be a good parent, etc. Or it could be simply someone to fill up the empty space inside you.

Now all of this is valid. However, it would benefit you to understand that this is so. If your partnerships, marriages or friendships are not as you would wish them to be, then you must look within to discover more about you and discover what beliefs and fears require attention.

If you want a relationship because of the fear of not being enough, it behooves you to look honestly at your beliefs and feelings. Again, pay attention. What do you believe about relationships and what do you believe about yourself in relationship.

Some of you may feel that you must be a certain way or be perceived to be the other person's ideal or even your own idea of what a "good wife" or "good husband" should be. This is fine for a time, but when you are not being who you really are, eventually the role begins to pall.

Honesty and vulnerability are the keys to intimacy and solid relationships. If you can really speak how you feel and be honest about your expectations and what you want for yourself, then you can learn about fair compromise and grow together as you learn more about each other. And it is never too late to start.

For some the idea of total honesty about who you are and what you really want is a scary proposition because opening up to that honesty requires you to be vulnerable. However being vulnerable is truly your greatest strength. If you can be open and vulnerable you are creating and allowing a safe space for your partner to be the same.

There is no place for hidden agendas, no room for manipulation and control. We see people feeling they must secretly manipulate to get what they want or use emotional blackmail or passive-aggression in what is an un-equal relationship.

We have spoken to people who are very unhappy in their marriage or partnership because they have discovered the spiritual path and their partner is either not interested or openly skeptical of this new direction. You know, you do not have to think the same way about everything. Where the basis of the relationship is love, then there is room for growth and change.

However, most of you have a vested interest in things remaining the same. For some, you will do almost anything to maintain the status quo. If one partner changes the rules, then sometimes the relationship will founder.

Some of you will stay in an unequal or unhappy situation through the fear of being alone or the fear of financial loss or loss of social position, etc. That is also valid. However, if you could actually deal with the fear of loss, you would find that either the relationship would change or you would not have the fear of loss holding you back from moving on.

This, of course, is not necessarily a bad thing. The idea of people having to stay is a relationship that is no longer viable is rather strange. Society and religion once used this idea as a way to control you. Some of you are still controlled by what others may think. We remind you that what other people think of you is not your business. All of you view each other through the lens of your own beliefs and judgments.

As you do not all expand and grow at the same time, you may find that you have or will move through different relationships in your life as you develop in different ways.

A good, if extreme, example of this would be to look at a hypothetical abusive relationship, perhaps a violent one. Now in an abusive relationship there is a deep and unspoken agreement between "perpetrator" and "victim." We have spoken of how you co-create your reality and this is an example.

The perpetrator, in the fear of being powerless and not enough, expresses those fears through aggression and violence. This person will co-create someone to play the role of victim. The victim, in the fear of being powerless and unworthy and believing that love equals pain, co-creates a partner to express this truth.

Then the victim says, "No! I am worth more than this. I will not tolerate this behavior any longer." Suddenly the rules have changed and the relationship cannot continue. The victim becomes sovereign and moves on to create a different life that will express the new idea or belief of who she/he is. The perpetrator, should she/he remain in the same state of being, will co-create another "victim" to play the game.

The more you discover about who you really are, the more you will make choices and decisions which reflect that knowing. Our desire for you is that you will expand and grow into deeper and more loving relationships with all people.

Love has nothing to do with ownership. Love has nothing to do with duty and "must" and "should." Love has nothing to do with social morality. Love is about the heart. Love is whole and complete in and of itself and requires no return. Love is just another name for Goddess/God, the All-That-Is. Love is the ultimate truth of who you really are.

11 PHYSICALITY

You created yourselves here in your body. You chose your particular body. It did not just happen. Without your body you would not be able to have this human experience. You chose your body in the same way that you chose your genetic heritage or your race.

Through the body you experience your physical world—see the beauty, hear the music, taste the delights of good food, smell the rose and touch your lover. What sensory delight!

Your body belongs to the Earth. Every component of your body is a component of the Earth herself. When you die, your consciousness moves on and the body returns to Earth where it belongs, whether it is as ash or a slower reduction of the cells. All is a cycle. Everything and everyone replenishes each other.

However, whilst the consciousness is in a way bound to the body, then the body reflects that consciousness. Where the mental and emotional bodies are healthy and balanced, the body will reflect this. We do not speak of those who have chosen to be birthed with some kind of physical impairment or genetic propensity to manifest a malfunction for this is chosen for that particular life-experience.

We have said that everything in the physical world is, in a way, a reflection of the non-physical. If there is a mental and/or emotional dis-easement, then you may expect that to manifest in some way in the physical body. It can be a challenging game to discover what the connection is.

The left side of the body represents feminine principle, interior life (perhaps hidden), and the right hemisphere of the brain, imagination and creative activity. The right side of the body represents masculine principle, exterior life (perhaps moving forward), and the left hemisphere of the brain, order and logic.

So if you were to have a dis-easement or injury only to the left or only to the right side of the body, then you would start to explore ideas around either principle and what that could represent in your life.

Each part of the body has functions or a purpose that may be transposed into the non-physical mental or emotional issues that need attention.

For example legs could represent mobility or moving forward. Are you afraid of moving on? Getting on with things? Do you feel stuck?

The knees could represent not only mobility, but also the ability or even necessity of bending. Are you being inflexible? The spine is your support. Have you forgotten that the Universe supports you absolutely? The blood or circulatory system is about flow and about life itself. The skin is what is between you and the rest of the world. How safe do you feel? It also holds everything together. How are you holding together?

You don't have to be rigid about this. It is not about getting it right. Whatever comes to mind may be the trigger for you to understand more about you. Often the body will reveal deeply held beliefs and even the conflict between what you know as a logical adult person and old beliefs or trauma carried over from childhood.

Your body is a miracle indeed. The complexity and synchronized orchestration of the body are awe-inspiring. Did you know that each cell of your body is a fractal of your universe? You could journey into a cell and watch the birth of a moon.

We are amazed at the negative thoughts most of you have about your bodies. Your society lays down an idea of what is "beauty" and so many rush to conform or condemn someone because she/he does not conform to this ideal. Or condemn yourselves for not being beautiful or handsome enough—too thin, too fat, too old.

Each of you, every one of you, has a unique beauty lit by the light of Divinity. We would very much enjoy to see you celebrate your body much more. Dance more! Become more aware of how the body feels to you. It would behoove you well to begin a very deep love affair with your body. Start really listening. Pay attention. Your body listens to every word you say, every thought, and feels every emotion. Why would your body serve you well if you do not love it, do not say "thank you" and do not treat it with consideration and common sense!

We notice that many of you on a spiritual path, and this includes many religions, in a way promote the idea that the body is not important. You should not pay too much attention to it. Or you need to subdue it because it can lead you astray and keep you from knowing God. Or indeed, get enlightened and ascend as quickly as you can and leave the damn thing behind!

Perhaps if you did not have so many issues around sexuality you would look more kindly on your body. You created yourselves here to really be here, in your body, to appreciate you in your world. To be here, not somewhere else. You are here to find happiness and fulfillment in your body, through which you can know and love the divine reflections of you, the miracles that surround you and the intensely vibrant experiences which you can only have through being in a body.

12 SEXUALITY

You are sexual beings from the moment of your birth until the moment of your death, even if you are not, for one reason or another, being physically sexual. Your sexuality is a real and valid facet of you, no matter how you express it.

Because of your social and collective consciousness, almost all of you think of your sexuality as separate from you. It is important that you realize you bring to the sexual facet of you the same thoughts and feelings that color the rest of your life.

Where your sense of self is balanced and you have learned how to deal with those fears and beliefs that limit and imprison you, then this will reflect in your sexual life as it does elsewhere in your life.

In your society you are not really taught about your sexuality. You may have learned the physical facts, but perhaps not about being sexual in its fullest sense. For many, there is a sense of shame around your sexuality. Some of you have been taught that sex is "dirty," your bodies unclean, or that you must "do your duty" without a thought that you might take pleasure in it.

In times past it was commonly thought that it is all right for men to enjoy sex but not women. These things may seem laughable in this age, but you as a society are still affected by these old beliefs.

In your society there is a certain ambivalence around children passing from childhood to sexual maturity. We see little celebration when a girl child begins her moon phases. There is more of an idea that this is something of a burden, being named "the curse" or other such names. It would be a wonderful thing if this time were to be celebrated as a Goddess event, a welcome to womanhood and a time for teaching about the joys and responsibilities of sex in a lighthearted and forthright manner.

Your boys do not have much of a celebration either, we see. Often these ones do not have much guidance or open discussion of what it means to be a man, not only in sexual terms, but in the way of teaching about honor and being the protector. One of the important roles for man to play is being the protector or guardian of the family and of the Earth herself and all things upon and within Her.

Most of the religions in your world have had a great part to play in your beliefs around sexuality. It is a great way to control you. You must only do it this way or that way. That way or this way is a sin. You must not have sex under these circumstances or those conditions.

Your sexuality was not designed simply for you to procreate. Not at all.

Rather, we would say, it is a grand game, not only as a most wonderful expression of love but also of play and fun and pleasure. Certainly to bring the fullness of love to the grand passion of sex may be sublime.

There is also much shame still associated with homosexuality in both men and women. The truth is that humankind was really created bi-sexual. Apart from the sex, we do remind you that love is love is love, wherever you find it. And sometimes you find love in the most unexpected places.

There is absolutely no judgment around homosexuality. If there are any rules about sex, and there really aren't, they would be these. In sex, as with any other interaction, you must treat the other person(s) with honor and respect and kindness. There must be a certain appropriate equality in a sexual relationship as with any other relationship. Honesty is important, too. You each bring your own preferences and desires to an encounter and as with any situation, the more of yourself you reveal, the more intimate and fulfilling the experience will be.

Of course sometimes you desire none of that. It is simply basic sex you want. This too is valid. You may have a snack instead of a banquet, but the same principals apply when you are dealing with anyone in any situation. Honor the sovereign being within each person as a reflection of who you are. No matter what games you play, sexual or otherwise, it is what is in your heart that is important.

13 DEATH

You are eternal. Death is not the end of anything. It is a transition. Your physical body returns to the Earth, to whom it belongs. Your consciousness returns to the Unified Field which, in a way, it has really never left, although you may not perceive that to be so.

Your death is as natural as your birth, and to describe what happens after death would be like trying to describe to a fetus in the uterus what life is like after birth. It does not fit into the box or structure of the consciousness of your reality.

Many of you are not so much afraid of death but the manner in which you may die. We remind you that you create your reality. At a very deep level it is you who chooses the place, time and manner of your death. As you become more in tune with who you are and your own power, you will nominate it as you please.

You know, the truth is that most of you die of a broken heart. We have said to you that the body will manifest physical dis-ease when the dis-ease of the mental and emotional embodiment is not healed. As you heal your wounded heart and create balance and more love and joy in your life, so you will come to a place where you may consciously choose when and how to depart your physical life.

When you come forth at birth, you have already chosen your game plan for this life. You choose a timeline for the game, yet this is not necessarily fixed but rather open to the possibility and probability factors. Some of you chose only to be in this life for a very short time. For some, the choice is to experience only the birth process itself. Some choose only to experience childhood in a chosen lifetime.

Always it is a sovereign choice. Sometimes you create events where the choice is to depart as a group, as in the instance of a "natural disaster," an airplane crash or some other mass event.

When you are in the midst of the grief of loss it behooves you to remember that each of you, no matter the circumstances, have had sovereign choice at the deepest level and that choice was to go Home. There is a rightness to that choice. Sometimes it is difficult to know that everything is always perfect.

Of course much of grief is that of the physical separation of a beloved. We do remind you that love means no separation. Nothing is truly separate. If you wish to be connected to the one who has gone, you may.

You all experience the connectedness in different ways. For some it is a feeling. For others it may be "hearing" or "seeing." All of it, no matter how it appears, is an affirmation that you are not really separate. Nothing is truly gone.

There is no negative Universal judgment about suicide. Suicide may be viewed as a cycle uncompleted. However it is to remember that simultaneously there is another lifetime being experienced where there is the opportunity to make different choices and to garner that particular wisdom. It is a valid choice, as is every other choice you make in your life. However, there are usually more harmonious choices, if only you could see it.

There are situations, such as what is perceived to be terminal illness, where suicide and even assisted suicide is chosen. This is a valid choice. Sometimes you simply tire of life as you are experiencing it and want it all to be finished. That also is valid. It is understood that you always do the best that you can in whatever circumstances you find yourself. Whatever you choose, you go Home.

When there is a horror story attached to death, you often get so caught up in the drama attached to the story that you forget that everything is a co-creation. This is particularly apparent where there has been a "victim" and a "perpetrator." This is not to condone or excuse the perpetrator of violent crime. It is to remind you that you are eternal beings playing this game called Life. Within every situation there is a gift. That gift is about the expansion of the heart and the deepening of understanding and compassion, not only for the victim, but for every person impacted by the situation. The recognition of sovereign choice and co-creation does not negate compassion.

Death is a gateway to new adventure. In a way you cast off your body as you would cast off your clothing at the end of a day. As you know that your clothing will be laundered and made new again, so your body will return to the Earth and be made new again and the Eternal You will go Home to create a new game.

Made in the USA
Charleston, SC
22 May 2013